Korean War
PUZZLE BOOK

CARLISLE, MASSACHUSETTS

Korean War Puzzle Book

Copyright © 2017 Applewood Books, Inc.

All rights reserved. No part of this book may be reproduced in any form or by any electronic or mechanical means without permission in writing from the publisher, except by a reviewer who may quote brief passages in a review.

ISBN: 978-1-945187-01-8

Published by
GRAB A PENCIL PRESS
an imprint of Applewood Books
Carlisle, Massachusetts
www.grabapencilpress.com

10 9 8 7 6 5 4 3 2 1

Manufactured in the United States of America

Korean War
PUZZLE BOOK

The Korean War was a conflict that arose from the end of World War II and resulted from Cold War hostilities between the United States and the Soviet Union. Korea had been ruled by Japan from 1910 until the end of World War II. At war's end the United States and Soviet Union agreed to divide Korea at the 38th parallel, separating the country into roughly two halves. The Democratic People's Republic of Korea (North Korea) was supported by the Soviet Union and People's Republic of China. The Republic of Korea (South Korea) had the support of the United States. Both governments felt that they represented the will of the entire Korean peninsula. The first president of the Republic of Korea, Syngman Rhee, was an anti-Communist strong-armed leader. The supreme leader of the People's Republic of Korea was Kim Il-sung. He sought the approval of Soviet leader Josef Stalin to invade South Korea to reunify the country. Because Stalin felt the United States did not have a strong interest in South Korea, he gave approval for North Korea to proceed.

Supported by both the Soviet Union and China, North Korean forces moved into South Korea June 25, 1950. The United Nations quickly demanded a cease-fire and authorized sending U.N. forces into Korea, made up mainly of military from the United States. After two months of fighting, South Korean troops backed by the U.N. forces were forced back to the Pusan Perimeter, a small corner of southeastern South Korea. Under the command of World War II hero General Douglas MacArthur, United Nations and South Korean forces decisively defeated North Korean forces at Inchon. North Korean and Chinese forces suffered heavy casualties. Battles and battle lines went back and forth, and South Korea's capital of Seoul changed hands four times. Korea was the first conflict in which air-to-air combat of jet fighters took place. While there was no decision in ground combat, Allied forces held air superiority in the bombing of North Korea.

The fighting came to an end July 27, 1953. The armistice signed by United Nations and North Korean military leaders ended fighting and established a Korean Demilitarized Zone separating North and South Korea. With no peace treaty the two countries remained at odds. The United States suffered 36,574 deaths on top of hundreds of thousands of North and South Koreans killed. Because the war was never declared and came to an end within three years of its start, it has been called the "Forgotten War." However, the war was brought back into America's consciousness with its depiction on *M*A*S*H,* the popular television series of the 1970s and '80s. The uneasy peace between North and South Korea continues to this day.

PUZZLE ANSWERS ON BACK PAGES

FLAG OF NORTH KOREA / KIM IL-SUNG

KOREA DIVIDED INTO OCCUPATION ZONES
– WIKIMEDIA COMMONS: USER: ELMO

Lead-up to War

ACROSS

3. The Autumn ___ of 1946 was organized by peasants in South Korea against the U.S. Army military government in Korea.

4. The U.S. Army military government was headed by General John R. ___.

7. Following Japan's defeat in WWII, the temporary division of North and South Korea at the 38th parallel was drawn at the ___ Conference.

8. North Korea supported the Communist ___ victory in 1949 and was supported by the People's Republic of China.

10. The Japan-Korea ___ Treaty of 1910 provided for Japan's rule over the Korean peninsula.

11. The People's ___ of Korea, lasting only one month, was formed after Japan surrendered, ending World War II in North Korea.

12. Soviet leader Josef ___ supported the invasion of South Korea by the North.

DOWN

1. After the defeat of the ___, ending World War II, the Korean peninsula was divided.

2. Syngman ___ was elected president of South Korea on July 20, 1948.

5. The Truman ___ of 1947 intended to provide U.S. help to any country under the Communist threat.

6. The ___ of at least 100,000 South Korean political prisoners thought to be Communists by the South Korean military, was blamed on North Korean Communists for forty years.

7. With Japan defeated, the U.S. and Soviet Union agreed to the 38th ___ being the political dividing line between North and South Korea in August 1945.

9. Supreme leader of North Korea Kim ___ was believed to have pushed for invasion of South Korea with Soviet support.

FLAG OF SOUTH KOREA / SYNGMAN RHEE

TROOPS OF THE THIRTY-FIRST INFANTRY REGIMENT LAND AT INCHON HARBOR, KOREA.

Battle of Inchon

ACROSS

4. United Nations and South Korean forces were led by U.S. Army General Douglas ___ at the Battle of Inchon.

5. The Battle of Inchon was an ___ invasion—by land and sea—was a victory for the United Nations.

10. The first elements of X Corps landed on the north side of Wolmido, named ___ Beach, on September 15, 1950.

11. Five days before the attack, napalm canisters were dropped on ___ to clear the way for American troops.

13. On September 17, 1950, North Korean aircraft dropped bombs on the U.S.S. ___, only one of which hit the craft, but it failed to detonate.

14. The First Marine Regiment landing at Inchon was led by Colonel Lewis "Chesty" ___.

DOWN

1. The Inchon invasion was code-named Operation ___.

2. ___ Beach, south of Inchon, was where the First Marine Regiment took the beachhead and road leading to Seoul.

3. A team from the Central ___ Agency was positioned at Inchon Harbor two weeks before the attack.

6. The North Koreans laid some naval ___ that a reconnaissance team removed during low tide before the invasion.

7. The successful victory at Inchon led to the recapture of the South Korean capital of ___ two weeks later.

8. The commander in chief of United Nations forces observed the attack on Inchon from the U.S.S. *Mount* ___ command ship.

9. The beach landings at Inchon were ___ -coded names.

12. South Korean troops used ladders to climb seawalls when landing at ___ Beach.

TROOPS AND ARMOR OF THE FIRST MARINE DIVISION MOVE THROUGH COMMUNIST CHINESE LINES AT THE CHOSIN RESERVOIR IN NORTH KOREA.

Battle of Chosin

ACROSS

2. North Korean forces and their outside support helped regain control of ___ Korea following the Chosin battle.

4. Major General Oliver P. ___ , of the First Marine Division, oversaw U.N. troops that were attacked by 120,000 Chinese troops at Chosin.

6. The result of the Chosin battle was the ___ of United Nations forces from North Korea.

10. The Chosin ___ Campaign was fought at a man-made lake on the northeastern part of the Korean peninsula.

12. The First, Fifth, Seventh, and Eleventh ___ Regiments defended positions in and around Chosin.

13. The complete withdrawal of U.N. troops from North Korea as a result of Chosin took place at the port of ___.

15. Chinese troops fighting at Chosin were under the command of ___ Shi Lun.

DOWN
1. The weather conditions were so harsh, ___ supplies froze during the battle.

3. The Chosin battle was fought during ___ weather conditions, with temperatures dropping to -35 degrees Fahrenheit.

5. United Nations troops were nicknamed "The Chosin ___."

7. The First Marine ___ Wing provided cover for U.N. forces at Chosin.

8. Major General Edward ___ commanded the U.S. X Corps at the Chosin battle.

9. Chairman Mao ___ of China ordered that the United Nations troops be destroyed at Chosin.

11. Some 120,000 ___ troops surrounded the United Nations forces at Chosin.

14. The X Corps at Chosin was made up of forces from the U.S. ___.

CROSSING THE 38TH PARALLEL – NARA

Multiple Choice

1. The reason the North Koreans began the war was __.
    a. to reunite North and South Korea as one nation
    b. to stop South Koreans from flooding into the North
    c. to stop North Koreans from flooding into the South
    d. to please Soviet leader Josef Stalin
    e. to anger the United States

2. North Korea's official name is the __.
    a. Communist People's Republic of Korea
    b. Democratic People's Republic of Korea
    c. Commonwealth of North Korea
    d. Republic of North Korea
    e. Crown Kingdom of North Korea

3. South Korea's official name is the __.
    a. Republic of Korea
    b. People's Republic of Korea
    c. Republic of South Korea
    d. South Korea
    e. Nationality of Korea

4. South Korea President Rhee ordered thousands in his country killed in June 1950, fearing they sided with the Communist North in what was called the __.
    a. South Korean Summer Massacre
    b. Unholy Killings
    c. Summer of 1950 Tragedy
    d. Summer of Terror
    e. Summer Slaughter

5. The Truman Doctrine of 1947 stated the advance of Communism anywhere in the world was a security threat ___.
    a. to the entire world
    b. to the United States
    c. to all democracies
    d. and was expected
    e. to be dealt with on a case-by-case basis

6. When the Korean conflict began, President Truman described it as ___.
    a. a riot
    b. a territorial dispute
    c. a military skirmish
    d. an armed uprising
    e. a police action

7. With the Korean armistice signed in July 1953, 1,500 square miles of territory was added to ___.
    a. the United Nations
    b. the People's Republic of China
    c. the Soviet Union
    d. South Korea
    e. North Korea

8. The percent of ___ casualties in the Korean conflict was higher than that of World War II or the Vietnam War.
    a. military
    b. Communist
    c. civilian
    d. American
    e. religious

9. Before and after the war, the 38th parallel of ___ was the approximate dividing line between North and South Korea.
    a. latitude
    b. longitude
    c. polarity
    d. meridian
    e. attitude

10. The Korean War has been called ___.
    a. the Unspoken War
    b. the Forgotten War
    c. the Mistaken War
    d. the Cold War
    e. the Unimportant War

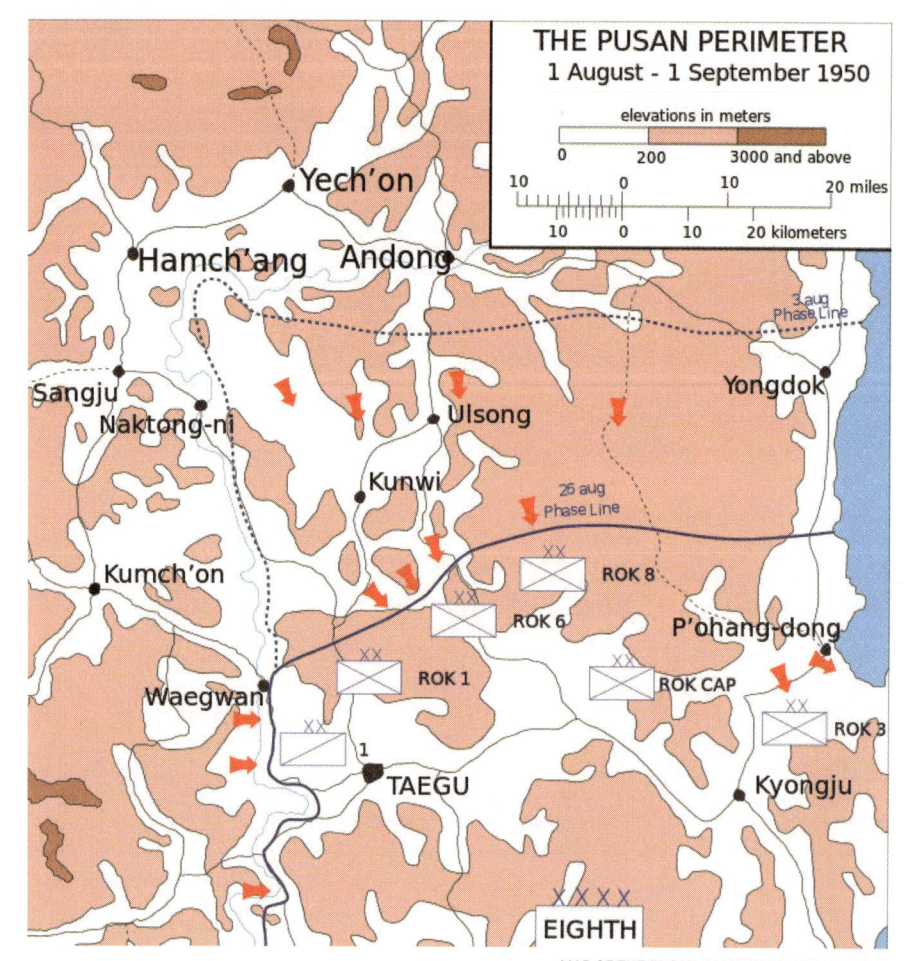

MAP OF THE PUSAN PERIMETER, AUGUST 1950
– CENTER FOR MILITARY HISTORY

Battle of Pusan Perimeter

ACROSS

1. Task Force ___, consisting of 20,000 men of the Twenty-Fifth Infantry Division, led one of the most successful defeats of the North Koreans.

6. The biggest challenge for U.N. forces was a shortage of ___.

7. ___ were the backbone of the transport system allowing U.N. troops to force a North Korean retreat.

9. North Korea's Fourth and Sixth ___ Divisions pushed back on U.S. and South Korean troops.

11. The Pusan Perimeter was the farthest ___ North Korean forces were able to penetrate into South Korea.

12. U.N. forces included troops from the ___ of South Korea.

DOWN

1. The last stand against North Korea was mounted by U.N. forces that included those from the United ___.

2. The United ___ forces consisted of 140,000 troops during the Pusan Perimeter battle in the summer of 1950.

3. The U.N. forces used the ___ terrain in the northern part of the perimeter as a natural defense against North Korean forces.

4. At its shorelines, the Pusan Perimeter extended from the Korean Strait to the Sea of ___.

5. The ___ general of the armed forces saw to it that rations from the U.S. were sent to U.N. troops at the Pusan battle.

8. Many U.N. casualties at Pusan resulted from intense summer heat and a severe ___.

10. U.N. forces were organized under the command of the U.S. ___.

KOREAN WAR SERVICE MEDAL

A VOUGHT F4U-4 CORSAIR FIGHTER BEING PREPARED FOR A MISSION

Korean Operations

ACROSS

1. Operation ___ was a United Nations offensive seizing the Chinese armies at the Jamestown line. (Military attack team member)

3. Operation ___ was a parachute drop of the 187th Airborne Combat Team ahead of the front line. (Cheer at Atlanta Braves games ending in "chop")

5. Operation Big ___ took place in August 1953, returning all prisoners of the Korean War. (It turns a light on or off)

6. Operation ___ was carried out by the U.S. Army, trapping North Korean and Chinese troops between two rivers. (Another word for brave)

7. Operation ___ was a February 1951 attack by U.S. X Corps on Pyongyang, North Korea. (Gathering cattle)

9. Operation Big ___ was a plan to destroy the Communist supply complex at Sibyon-ni. (A broken-off tree branch)

12. Operation ___ was a February 1952 tactic to trick the Communists by silence along the front lines for five days. (Keep one's mouth shut)

13. Operation ___ was an offensive against the North Koreans at Ch'unch'on. (One who tears paper up)

15. Operation ___ brought direct fire to enemy bunkers and artillery inaccessible to other mortar fire. (Tall chest of drawers on legs)

16. Operation ___ bombed North Korean railroads. (Moisten completely)

DOWN

2. Operation ___ was an attempt by U.S.A.F. pilots to get Communist pilots of MiG-15 jet fighters to defect to South Korea. (Slang term for money)

4. Operation Blue ___ was an American amphibious landing at Pohang by the First Cavalry Division. (Valentine's Day symbols)

5. Operation ___ was a 1951 air operation to disrupt North Korean logistics by bombing. (Choke someone)

6. Operation ___ was a surprise sea assault by 75,000 troops that resulted in the recapture of Seoul, South Korea. (An iron oxide mineral)

8. Operation ___ was a final major counterattack to destroy Chinese lines around the Iron Triangle. (Professional wrestling move)

10. Operation ___ was conducted by Allies to gain control of Heartbreak Ridge. (A way to score in football)

11. Operation ___ was an X Corps offensive by U.N. forces against the Chinese and North Korean forces. (A murderer)

14. Operation ___ was an emergency shipment of logistical materiel from the U.S. to the Far East in support of the war. (A shade of red)

GENERAL MACARTHUR INSPECTS TROOPS AT KIMPO AIRFIELD

Word Scramble

```
C N O H C N I O S H D I C K E L
A H S U E T R G N A Y G N O Y P
T I O N R I U H O U A M E H F A
W L G S D R H E E B S Y N R U G
I C H G I A T V N R U I Y E T P
S E W O M N R I C T L O K A U M
H A N C R E A S H A E T W S H I
Y N O R V I C O T R U M A N R E
L E I H C S A S N A M N Y E C A
A S T A L E M A T E R I A B O W
T G U S O N R G H O K S W N U S
E N H T S H A F N S C O Y T E P
K O R E A O C E L U M N A O B I
A D E R B W H I R E S G U L A N
P E M U D E V T F A O L K H R T
R Z I K O R E L U P H E I E C S
```

Find the following:

PUSAN
CHOSIN
PYONGYANG
SEOUL
RHEE
MACARTHUR
INCHON
SONG
ZEDONG
STALIN
TRUMAN
IL-SUNG
RIDGWAY
EISENHOWER
KOREA
STALEMATE

Sudokus

ARMY

M			Y
		R	
			A
A	Y		

GROUND CREW MEMBERS OF THE THIRD BOMB WING WORK ON A U.S. AIR FORCE B-26 NIGHT INTRUDER. – NARA

U.S.A.F.

	S		F
F			
S			A
	U		

KOREAN

R					
		O		A	
K	E	O			
N			A		
				A	
	E		R		K

CHOSIN

	O		N		
	C				H
				O	N
N		O	S		
				H	S
H	I		C		

STRANGLE

L	T			R		S		
		E						
	A				G			
	E	S		A				L
A					E		T	
	L		E	N		S		
		R						
G					S		R	

PUNCHBOWL

	L		O		P		W	
P					C			N
	U	B		H		L		P
	N	O			W	H		B
		L	H				N	
W			B					O
	B		N			P		L
	P			C	L			
	W	U		O			C	H

M*A*S*H SIGN

M*A*S*H

ACROSS

2. MASH stands for Mobile Army Surgical ___.

4. Wayne Rogers played Captain "___" John McIntyre for the first three seasons of the show.

7. Head nurse Major Margaret ___ was played by Loretta Swit.

8. The *M*A*S*H* commanding officer was seen driving a ___ Jeep M38A1.

11. ___ Pierce, played by Alan Alda, was the star and chief surgical captain.

13. Surgical Captain B. J. ___, played by Mike Farrell, was a character from season four through season eleven.

14. From dressing in skirts to company clerk, Corporal/Sergeant Max ___ was played by Jamie Farr.

16. Called "Padre" by Harry Morgan, Father ___ was the chaplain of the 4077th.

6. ___, South Korea, was the location of the 4077th during the war.

DOWN

1. The last episode, February 28, 1983, "Goodbye, ___ & Amen" was the most-watched television event (125 million viewers) up to that time.

3. Story lines in early seasons of the show were based upon accounts from real MASH ___.

5. Alan Alda and Jamie Farr served in the U.S. ___ in Korea after the war.

9. The Bell H-13 ___ helicopter was the model used for the landing of wounded at the 4077th.

10. Colonel Sherman ___, played by Harry Morgan, commanded the 4077th unit.

12. M*A*S*H aired on CBS while the ___ War was being battled.

15. Company clerk and bugler Corporal "___" O'Reilly was played by Gary Burghoff for eight seasons.

A U.S. ARMY BELL H-13 IN FRONT OF A U.S. AIR FORCE CURTISS C-46 COMMANDO IN KOREA, 1952. – NARA

Korean War Aircraft

ACROSS

2. In an airlift role, the Curtiss C-46 ___ supplied aircraft engines, ammunition, medical supplies, and rations.

4. The Boeing B-17 ___ Fortress replaced its bombing equipment with photographic equipment for mapping purposes.

5. The Military Air Transport Service workhorse and the first U.S.A.F. aircraft destroyed in the war while on the ground was the C-54 ___.

8. The B-26 ___ flew the first and last bombing missions and was valued for its night-flying ability.

9. Many B-29 ___ were retrieved from storage; together they dropped 167,000 tons of bombs during the war.

13. The Republic F-84E ___ was used for attacking such enemy ground targets as airfields and irrigation dams.

14. While inferior to the enemy MiG fighters, the F-80C ___ Star was successful in clearing the skies of North Korean aircraft.

DOWN

1. The C-119 Flying ___ aided in the retreat of Marine Corps and army troops from Chosin Reservoir.

3. The transport of heavy loads of cargo to and from Korea was handled by the C-124 ___ II.

5. Because the Lockheed F-94B ___ carried a secret radar system on board, it was kept from flying deep into enemy territory.

6. The U.S.A.F. F-86 ___ was the most successful fighter of the war, shooting down 792 enemy MiG fighters.

7. F-51D ___ jet fighters were outdated but useful in landing on the short airstrips in North Korea.

10. Used primarily for reconnaissance, the four-jet RB-45 ___ bomber flew out of an air base in Japan.

11. Nicknamed the "Gooney Bird," the C-47 ___ dropped paratroopers, hauled supplies, and evacuated the wounded.

12. The ___ H-13 Sioux helicopter was used to transport wounded soldiers to MASH units.

SERGEANT RECKLESS AT CAMP PENDLETON, 1959

Korean War Facts

ACROSS

2. The U.S. Army used an estimated 1,500 ___ in the Korean War, whereas about 4,000 were used in the Vietnam War.

5. Korea was considered the first military action of the ___ War period.

7. The war was considered a ___ action because President Truman never asked Congress for a declaration of war.

8. Before reaching the battlefield, many soldiers died of ___ due to weather conditions.

10. South Korea refers to the war as the 6-2-5 ___, as the date the North invaded the South was June 25, 1950.

11. A total of 635,000 tons of ___ were dropped during the Korean War, more than the amount used in the Pacific during WWII.

12. Because peace was uncertain, Congress extended the war period to January 1955 to provide ___ for soldiers.

13. The state of ___ has the greatest number of Korean War veterans at 430,800.

DOWN
1. The South Korean capital of ___ changed hands four times during the war.

3. The horse named Sergeant ___ carried ammunition to soldiers on the Korean battlefield.

4. The first all-jet ___ occurred during the Korean War on September 8, 1950.

5. A ___-fire was signed July 27, 1953, as there was no official treaty ending the war.

6. Seven percent of the veterans of the Korean War (86,300) were ___.

9. Ninety percent of the fighting troops in defense of South Korea were ___.

Weaponry of the Korean War

1. M1A1 Carbine ___
2. M2HB Browning Machine Gun ___
3. 155mm Long Tom ___
4. M1 Bazooka ___
5. M1917 Revolver ___
6. M2 Mortar ___
7. Thompson M1928 Machine Gun ___
8. M1911 Pistol ___
9. M1903 Springfield Rifle ___
10. 240mm Howitzer M1 ___

A

B

C

CREDIT: JASON LONG

D

CUNEO

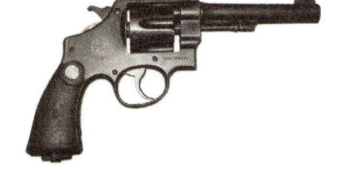

E

WIKIMEDIA COMMONS – USER: RAMA

F

WIKIMEDIA COMMONS – USER: STEFAN KÜHN

G

WIKIMEDIA COMMONS – USER: CURIOSANDRELICS

H

I

J

WIKIMEDIA COMMONS – USER: ВИТАЛИЙ БАРСОВ

A BLACK-PAINTED U.S. AIR FORCE DOUGLAS B-26C INVADER DROPS BOMBS. – NARA

True or False

Circle the correct answer to the statements below.

1. The Korean War was the first military action during the Cold War period. TRUE FALSE

2. President Truman, with the approval of Congress, declared war on North Korea and the Chinese. TRUE FALSE

3. Seoul, the capital of South Korea, changed hands ten times during the course of the war. TRUE FALSE

4. The Korean War was the first conflict in which Mobile Army Surgical Hospitals were deployed. TRUE FALSE

5. A German shepherd named Sergeant Reckless helped marines during the war carrying ammunition to the field of action. TRUE FALSE

6. The surgical hospital camp that was made famous by the television show *M*A*S*H* was located in North Korea. TRUE FALSE

7. More bombs were dropped during the Korean War than were used in the Pacific Theater in World War II. TRUE FALSE

8. There were 33,686 American combat deaths in the Korean War. TRUE FALSE

9. The United Nations supported North Korea and the People's Republic of China during the Korean War. TRUE FALSE

10. Instead of a treaty officially ending the war, a cease-fire was signed by each side. TRUE FALSE

PUZZLE ANSWERS

Lead-up to War

Battle of Inchon

Battle of Chosin

Multiple Choice

1. a
2. b
3. a
4. d
5. b
6. e
7. d
8. c
9. a
10. b

Battle of Pusan Perimeter

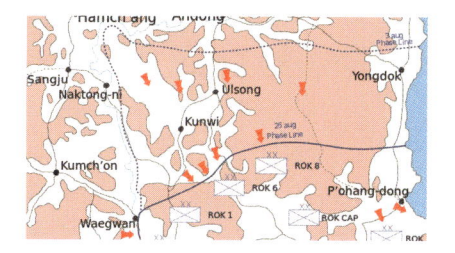

Korean Operations

					K	E	A	N	
M		J		Q	I			A	
O	A	M	M	U	N	I	T	I	O	N
U		P		A	G			I	
N		R	A	I	L	R	O	A	D	S
T		N		T	D			O	
A				E	O			N	
I	N	F	A	N	T	R	Y		S	
N		R		M	U				
O		M		A	G				
U		Y		S	O	U	T	H	E	A	S	T
S				T					
				E					
				R	E	P	U	B	L	I	C

					C	O	M	M	A	N	D	O
					O							
					T	O	M	A	H	A	W	K
					L		E					
			S	W	I	T	C	H	A			
					T			R				
C	O	U	R	A	G	E	O	U	S			
H									S			
R	O	U	N	D	U	P		S	T	I	C	K
O				I			O		I	L	L	E	R
M			C	L	A	M	-	U	P	
R	I	P	P	E	R		C			
T				D		H			
E				R		D			
	H	I	G	H	B	O	Y			
			V		W					
S	A	T	U	R	A	T	E			

Word Scramble

C	N	O	H	C	N	I	O	S	H	D	I	C	K	E	L
A	H	S	U	E	T	R	G	N	A	Y	G	N	O	Y	P
T	I	O	N	R	I	U	H	O	U	A	M	E	H	F	A
W	L	G	S	D	R	H	E	E	B	S	Y	N	R	U	G
I	C	H	G	I	A	T	V	N	R	U	I	Y	E	T	P
S	E	W	O	M	N	R	I	C	T	L	O	K	A	U	M
H	A	N	C	R	E	A	S	H	A	E	T	W	S	H	I
Y	N	O	R	V	I	C	O	T	R	U	M	A	N	R	E
L	E	I	H	C	S	A	S	N	A	M	N	Y	E	C	A
A	S	T	A	L	E	M	A	T	E	R	I	A	B	O	W
T	G	U	S	O	N	R	G	H	O	K	S	W	N	U	S
E	N	H	T	S	H	A	F	N	S	C	O	Y	T	E	P
K	O	R	E	A	O	C	E	L	U	M	N	A	O	B	I
A	D	E	R	B	W	H	I	R	E	S	G	U	L	A	N
P	E	M	U	D	E	V	T	F	A	O	L	K	H	R	T
R	Z	I	K	O	R	E	L	U	P	H	E	I	E	C	S

Sudokus

ARMY

M	R	A	Y
Y	A	R	M
R	M	Y	A
A	Y	M	R

U.S.A.F.

U	S	A	F
F	A	S	U
S	F	U	A
A	U	F	S

KOREAN

R	N	A	K	E	O
E	K	O	N	A	R
K	A	E	O	R	N
N	O	R	A	K	E
O	R	K	E	N	A
A	E	N	R	O	K

CHOSIN

S	O	H	N	I	C
I	C	N	O	S	H
C	S	I	H	O	N
N	H	O	S	C	I
O	N	C	I	H	S
H	I	S	C	N	O

STRANGLE

L	T	G	N	E	R	A	S
S	R	E	A	T	L	N	G
T	A	L	R	S	N	G	E
N	E	S	G	A	T	R	L
A	G	N	S	R	E	L	T
R	L	T	E	N	G	S	A
E	S	R	L	G	A	T	N
G	N	A	T	L	S	E	R

PUNCHBOWL

N	L	H	O	U	P	B	W	C
P	O	W	L	B	C	U	H	N
C	U	B	W	H	N	L	O	P
U	N	O	C	L	W	H	P	B
B	C	L	H	P	O	W	N	U
W	H	P	B	N	U	C	L	O
O	B	C	N	W	H	P	U	L
H	P	N	U	C	L	O	B	W
L	W	U	P	O	B	N	C	H

M*A*S*H

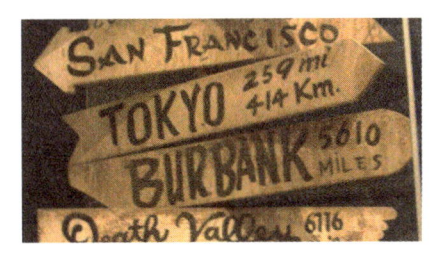

```
        F
H O S P I T A L
    U   R
    T R A P P E R
    G   W     A
    E   E     R
    O   L     M
U   O   L     
H O U L I H A N S    W I L L Y S    P
  J                      I        O
  H A W K E Y E      V   O        T
  O           H U N N I C U T T   T
  K L I N G E R      E   X        E
    G       A        T            R
    B       D        N
    M U L C A H Y    A
            R        M
```

Korean War Aircraft

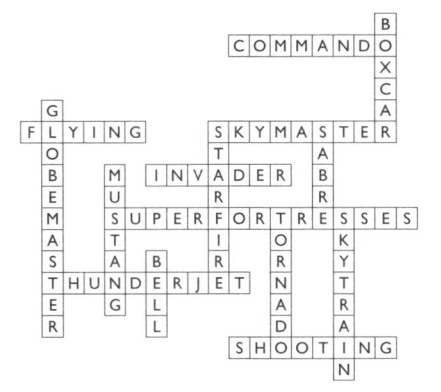

```
                              B
            C O M M A N D O
                              O
                              X
                              C
        G                     A
F L Y I N G    S K Y M A S T E R
        O          T          A
        B   M   I N V A D E R B
        E   U    R            R
        M   S U P E R F O R T R E S S E S
        A   T    I    O       K
        S   A B  R    R       Y
        T H U N D E R J E T   T
        E   G    L    A       R
        R        L    D       A
                 S H O O T I N G
```

Korean War Facts

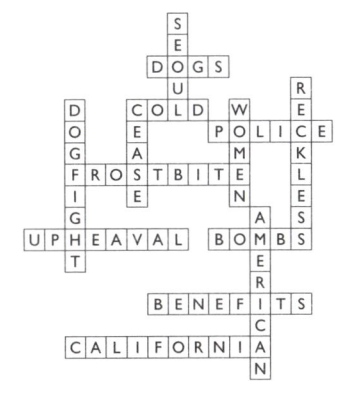

```
        S
        E
      D O G S
        U         R
  D   C O L D W   E
  O   E     P O L I C E
  G   A     M     K
    F R O S T B I T E
        E    N    E
             A    S
U P H E A V A L B O M B S
  T                  E
                     R
        B E N E F I T S
                     C
  C A L I F O R N I A
                     N
```

Weaponry of the Korean War

1. d
2. i
3. j
4. a
5. e
6. g
7. f
8. b
9. h
10. c

True or False

1. True. Following WWII, the Cold War "war of words" between the U.S. and Soviet Union was interrrupted by the Korean War.

2. False. The Korean War was undeclared and considered a police action by President Truman.

3. False. Seoul changed hands between North and South four times during the conflict.

4. True. The first MASH units were established by the U.S. Army in August 1945, but they were not deployed until the Korean conflict.

5. False. Sergeant Reckless was a decorated horse honored for her accomplishments in the battlefield of Korea.

6. False. The 4077th MASH unit on the television show was located in Uijeongbu, South Korea.

7. True. A total of 635,000 tons of bombs were dropped on North Korea, whereas about 500,000 tons fell in the Pacific during WWII.

8. True. The U.S. suffered 33,686 combat deaths out of 36,574 total (combat and noncombat) deaths.

9. False. The United Nations, led largely by U.S. troops, supported the South Koreans during the war.

10. True. On July 27, 1953, an armistice ending all hostilities was signed by the United Nations Command and North Korea.

TOPICS
GRAB A PENCIL PRESS

Abraham Lincoln	National Parks
American Flag	Natural History
American Revolution	New York City
Architecture	Presidents of the United States
Art History	Secret Writing
Benjamin Franklin	Texas History
Black History	Thanksgiving
California Gold Rush	Vietnam War
Civil War History	Washington, D.C.
Ellis Island and the Statue of Liberty	Women's History
First Ladies	World War II
George Washington	World War II European Theater
John Fitzgerald Kennedy	World War II Pacific Theater
Korean War	Yellowstone National Park

COMING SOON
Flight Puzzle Book
Library of Congress Puzzle Book

an imprint of Applewood Books
Carlisle, Massachusetts 01741
www.grabapencilpress.com

To order, call: 800-277-5312